magic of the modest

poems by

r.c. perez

ISBN: 978-1-7776334-0-0 (Print)
ISBN: 978-1-7776334-1-7 (eBook)

Illustrations by Angela Dianne Agustin - @frstlovenvrdice
Front cover image by Van Piedad - @thoughtelage
Cover design by Booklerk

ignovionwrites@gmail.com
@ignovionwrites

introduction

In this world that has too quickly become too complex, too loud, and often too unforgiving, it is easy to be overwhelmed and miss the joy of simple things around us.

This book is about those simple things—and the magic we find in them.

It is divided into four chapters, with each chapter taking its title from a Filipino word or concept, as an homage to the poetic beauty of Philippine languages.

Chapter 1 is called *Padayon* (to continue). It explores the themes of loss, longing, and heartaches, and the magic in carrying on.

Chapter 2 is called *Paglaom* (aspiration). It deals with topics of hopes, dreams, and aspirations, and the magic in looking forward to things.

Chapter 3 is titled *Tawhay* (state of being relaxed, at peace, without worry). Poems in this chapter talk about different forms of acceptance, self-love, and inner peace, and the magic in letting it be.

Finally, Chapter 4 is titled *Hiwaga* (mystery). Through the poems in this chapter, readers experience the mystery and magic of love, in all its many kinds.

Tied together, these chapters take readers to a journey of pain, hope, acceptance, and love—one that is all too familiar to anyone who has had a bit of experience in life.

But while this book was written with people in the same generation as I am in mind, I am certain that younger readers, as well as the generations ahead, will find something in here that strikes a chord in their hearts because, at one point, we all have felt the magic of the modest.

I hope you feel it in here, too.

table of contents

"And above all, watch with glittering eyes the whole world around you because the greatest secrets are always hidden in the most unlikely places."

—— Roald Dahl

for you—
you are magical

padayon

CHAPTER 1

of loss,
longing,
heartaches,
and moving on

A Place

Why is it
that we may hang our coats
and still not call it home?

Why is it
that we may sit around the table,
laugh at each other's jokes
and still feel alone?

There must be a place
where we belong.
This can't be
all there is.

Battles We Don't Tell

How many times
have the four walls
of your room
seen you break
like no one ever would?

At night, what does
the ceiling see
as it stares right
into your soul?

And which of all
your pain and sorrow
do the curtains
hide from the world?

When you go out, nobody
—nobody ever knows.

Lull

When it's late at night
I like to turn on the music
and sing my demons to sleep.

Sleepless

Could it be possible
that we've already had
the best days of our lives?
And all these sleepless nights
are just for stalling,
knowing deep inside
that every tomorrow
will never get any better
no matter how hard we try?

Home
is half a world
away.

Monster Within

Your inner saboteur is growing strong.
In the darkest corner inside your head,
it looms, feeds off of your regrets—
what should and should not have been said.
It drinks from every drop of hope in you,
that things always work out in the end,
if you let them be. The claws it brandishes
are sharpened by the blades of lies
and excuses you keep telling yourself.
Overthinking is its name
and isn't it just a relentless monster.
Starve it to death and never let it win.

Weightless

Of course, I glide
when walking.
After all,
it isn't so hard
to carry oneself
when inside,
there is nothing.

Silent Storms

There are storms
that make the quietest sound—
no howling winds or thundering rains.
There are storms that destroy
without famine or floods.
Yet just as unrelenting,
just as unabashed,
they can drown you.
Over and over they will leave you
breathless but alive.

They are the ones we harbor
inside of us.

Never Not Flowing

This isn't death,
for I shall live
through thousand
winters more.

I am a river,
cold and frozen,
and I shall live again.

Beneath the surface,
quietly
I still flow.

The Other Kind

Strength resides in you.
Most days,
it's meant for war;
sometimes,
it's simply for survival.

There is no shame
in calling it a day.
Even the strongest beasts
know when it's time
for deep slumber,
but they always,

always,
come back
to life.

Conditioning

I can't wait
to write a sad poem
about you.

Runners

Won't we ever
tire of this?
People come,
people go.

Everybody's running—
some in circles,
some toward,
some away
from something.

Last

One last time—
you, tonight with me,
and tomorrow,
a memory.

Hiding in the Haze

Kiss me before
the fog fades away.
Hold me while there's
nobody to stare—
all the things
we couldn't do
when the world was clear.

Engulfed by
the morning haze,
we only have
each other.

In the thickness of it all,
we could pretend
nothing else matters.

The Price We Pay

Break my heart
and be worth
all the pain.

For is it even
love at all
if it isn't worth
hurting for?

The Nights We Burn

How could we not admire
this glowing ember
amidst all the ashes
of the night we just burned?

Dawn is peeking and the cold
has hummed its way here.
But it still burns, albeit faintly,
and how could we not think
that it's all for the words
still left unsaid, and hands
waiting to be held?

How foolish will we be
if we wasted this generosity.

Bubble Gum

Your love
is bubble gum in my mouth
of which I cannot seem
to get enough.

The taste has gone
a long while,
but I keep on chewing,
not much for the sweetness
my tongue can no longer find,
but for the comfort of the familiar
every time my teeth grind.

Hushed

When the rain starts to pour
do you hear my words
whispered amidst the sound
of the raindrops as they
kiss the ground?

When the rain stops
do you feel by the way
the wind blows
how heavy it is with words hushed
as it carries them back to me?

Shades of Lies

All those times I was smitten by your words,
if only for one second I squinted my eyes,
if I tilted my head,
I'm sure I would have noticed behind you
waving were all the red flags
in all shades of your lies.

Spin

Sometimes it was as if
we were only spinning
inside these songs,
in the lyrics you forced to fit.
And I couldn't get out.

Were we only living in the fantasy
of your favorite songs?
Hereon and always, there will be
songs that will remind me of you.

But the thing about believing
your life is a love song
is that when the music stops,
you realize you never had
a melody of your own.

Phobia Talk

I am afraid of the rain, I said,
how it always comes uninvited,
how just as quickly as it appears,
it vanishes.
I am afraid of love, you said.
Same thing, I replied.

Dead as a Flower

Memories of you—
preserved like dead flowers
pressed in between the pages
of a forgotten book,
just fragile remnants
of something wonderful
—scents of love
that once filled a room.

Bit Too Soon

Candy-coated lie
—one bite and out
came dripping,
a bitter truth
covered inside.

Reverse

Stuck in this mania,
in *retromarcia*.
I keep finding myself
coming back to you.

The Prey

Do not blame yourself
for being lured
into the woods,
where monsters made
a feast out of you.

When it is dark
and all you want
is a place of warmth,
all the flickering lights
look like home to you.

Autumn Special

I remember a day
when the room smelled
of pumpkin spice,
how we both
couldn't hide our disgust.

But we had a taste of it,
anyway. And then,
the craze was gone.

And maybe, for you and me,
what we had, that's also
all it ever was—
a fleeting, frivolous fad.

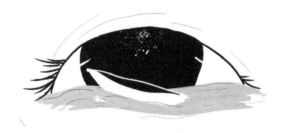

When the Sailing Was Smooth

Grief comes in waves,
in treacherous fashion.
Sail long enough
and it's easy to think
you have mastered
the art of maneuver.

Then the big one arrives
to devour you alive.

Shell

I picked up a shell on the shore
hoping to hear your voice inside,

because I once read somewhere,
those who loved and were loved
never really die—
they come back as magic,

because I am learning
there is no longing
quite as painful
as missing the sound
of your laughter in the flesh.

And Now There Remain

What, if not hope,
do we hold on to?

Where, if not from each other,
do we draw strength?

How, if not with unwavering faith,
do we look forward to better days?

Always Someone

It has always terrified me
to think that nobody
will ever know my pain.
But when I stretch my arms
and my hands bud open
like flowers in the spring
to catch the first drop of rain,
I get shivers
from a strange familiarity.
Then I breathe in—
and find solace in the certainty
that it is the very same tear
that has once dried on my cheek.

paglaom

CHAPTER 2

of hopes,
dreams,
and aspirations

Giver

And all this love
you give—
someday,
somehow,
someplace else
you will receive,
and more.

On Hold

Delayed, derailed,
detoured perhaps;
stuck on the road,
but there is no
turning back.

The light will soon
turn green and
onward we go, chasing
the many things
we are bound to do
and yet to become.

--pandemic poem #1

Fire—
your eyes,
warm and wild.
May you never lose
the wonder of a child.

Biopic

Spoiler—
we die in the end.
So what?
Play your life, anyway
—play it loud, do not
skip even just
one second of it.
There is no rewind.

Pause if............

it gets too much,
and then, resume.
Enjoy it; stay put
for the credits.
Take a look, one last time,
at the cast that made
your blockbuster
of a life possible,
all the people
you are thankful for.

Sunset
reminds us
that some things
can still end beautifully,
with promise of new beginnings.

The Greatest Wordsmith

I have forged
a million words
into poems, all for
the wrong people.

But I am a wordsmith,
and forge I will.
I shall stay close
to the warmth of this fire
until I find you.

Imagine,
what my anvil hand
can craft for you
—-the one.
Imagine.

You are a masterpiece
waiting to come
into existence.

Script

Conversations
inside my head,
in these made-up
scenarios and
make-believe tales.

When I am here,
I always know
just what to say.

The One Who Wonders

I had a thought,
a wild and wondrous one,
that somewhere far off
there is a place
where what the heart speaks
is echoed by the mind.

Imagine bliss,
imagine freedom.

I had this thought,
and it may very well be
just a wishful, whimsical one.

But if by chance
you come across a wanderer
who knows the way
to this wonderland,
would you be kind enough
to tell them about a dreamer
whose only wish is to fly?

Firefly

Lightning bug
above your head,
and marvel, inside it.
When will you ever
chase that glowing
light of wonder?

Follow,
follow the firefly—
into the woods,
and through the dark.
Who knows what magic,
what mystery,
what other world
it wants you to see.

Who knows.
Only the brave
ever find out.

When You Love

But when you love,
love not with hands
that tightly grasp.
Clenched fists
are for war.

Love with open palms,
with the tenderness
of offering hands.

For love gives
more than it takes.

Love gives freedom.
Love is freedom.

Another World

When things around you
get cold, remember,
there is another world.

Fly,
fly away from here.
Find all the warmth
and fill your heart with it.

I Am Yet to Write My Favorite Poem

I am yet to write
my favorite poem.
There will be
no grandeur, nor
a spectacular
display of words.
It will be devoid
of verses, rhymes,
and rhythm.

But believe me,
it will be magic—
all at once
magnificent and mundane.

When the time comes,
I know I will grab my pen,
uncrumple a piece of paper
and on there, there, I will write

your name.

Skin Hunger

But our fingers are made
to brush against
somebody else's skin.
These arms of ours
are meant for long
and warm embrace.

Take me back to the time
when it wasn't sin
to hunger for skin.

--pandemic poem #2

The Waiting

It is not so much
of what comes after the waiting.
Sometimes, it's the waiting itself,
the looking forward to things,
when you feel your blood running
through your whole body, heart
beating fast, hands trembling
in yearning anticipation.

And for once,
you might have believed
you were living.

Tell me not,
when there was nothing else,
hope did not keep you alive.

So many lives
I couldn't live;
so many worlds
I will never see.

Give me poetry.
Let me in;
let me *be*.

Things I Missed

The blue night bus, one cold North York
November night. The chance to ask for
the stranger's name, at the stop. The alarm.
Early morning classes. The fun. That time
somebody probably said, *This is already the
best days of our lives.* Calls. Shots I didn't take.
Half of my life. Whatever *never mind* really
meant. Opportunities to speak up. A beat.
The point. Punchlines. Deadlines. Subtle
hints. Easter eggs. Freeway exits, because
I always drive and daydream. The target.
Many, many chances at love.

Recipe for Hope

one cup
a spoonful
one sip
a smile at the void
two shots
one spirited sigh

If only we could measure hope,
if only the heart knows limits, if only.
This is what the break of day looks,
when coffee tastes marvelous
and hope overflows.

Paper Folding

I hope you find courage
to embrace
all your endless possibilities.

I hope you realize
you can become
the most stunning work of art.

to love and
be loved
quietly,
steadily,
constantly

Lucky Leaf

Tell me,
how many first days of autumn
did you spend sitting under a tree,
hoping to catch the first falling leaf
for that one fervent wish?

I hope you finally figured out
you could always shake the branches
and shower in all the luck
you made yourself.

What Time Is It?

But what is time for
other than to remind us
we ought to be
somewhere else?

Measure life in moments
that make you forget
all other things exist.

I Wish to Be the Water

If you don't get to see me again,
the raindrops will hold memories
of us together. Do not come out;
do not try to catch every little
bit of me with cupped hands.

Instead, let it nourish the earth;
let the seeds sprout;
let the wild grass grow.

When the drizzle disappears,
I do not wish to be
scattered droplets of happy and sad,
of silly and mad, left on your palms
that you'll have to dry.

I wish to be the water
that makes others feel alive.

Collecting Bullets

And they kept firing
all those bullets
your way, so certain
they would shatter you.

One thing they didn't know,
you are an alchemist.
You turn metal
into gold.

Overflowing

Lucky are those
who plant kindness
like seeds all around,
for they will reap
all that they sow
come harvest time
—a cornucopia
of overflowing love.

Love Brought Us Here

Many years from now,
when battles
have been fought
and love
has finally won,
someone will whisper this
in their lover's ear,
with much pride
and gratitude:

Thank you for believing in us.

The Existence

If a tree falls in a forest
and I am the only one
around to hear it,
I hope I will remember
what sound it makes,
so I could tell everyone
it did, indeed, exist.

Parade of Leaves

In the faintest yellows
I saw gentle surrender,
in the brightest reds
I saw burning hope.
And somewhere in
between, a simple truth:
for every leaf that falls,
something new
is coming along.

A Paradise to Share

How absolutely lucky for you and me
to get to share this world and all its beauty
with the birds in the sky that know
the secrets of the earth from up above,
and all the creatures beneath the oceans
that have swum all unknown corners below,
long before we learned to walk on land.

How absolutely mundane our existence
compared to theirs, and I have a feeling,
if we look at things this way, we will never
again think so highly of ourselves, that we
will know this world as a paradise to share,
and not a kingdom to rule.

I would like to believe
all that matters in the end
is how graciously we lived.

Take Me Anywhere

Take me into the deepest jungle
inside your soul,
grown from years and years of yearning.
Tell me about the monsters I need to tame
and I will tell the story over and over,
under my breath like muffled prayer,
until it becomes a promise, until you know
the wait is over.

Take me to the castles you built
out of the broken pieces of love you lost.
Some days, I will wonder what marvel there is
in staring at such fragile majesty.
Some days, I will ponder on how it's both burden
and privilege to know how they once were shattered.
Remind me then how easily they could crumble.

Take me anywhere with you
far and beyond reach, until finding home
is nothing but a wish we once made,
until it's but a hazy memory
of the days when we were scared.

My feet are aching for an adventure
and I am ready to get lost.

of acceptance,
self-love,
and inner peace

Unapologetic

And when the sunset
casts a golden shadow
along the horizon,
there is no telling
how many eyes
stare in admiration.

It does not know
how not to be
beautiful.

Believe in Magic...

because if you just try hard enough,
you will feel the way the trees trade
breaths of life with you, or hear
the faintest heartbeat of the animals
sleeping soundly underneath
the snow-covered ground, and then
you'll realize, it is not too hard
to understand that this world
is a wonderful, magical paradise.

There is magic in the ordinary—
in the way no two snowflakes are alike;
in the way my phone beeps just as
I thought of you; in the way you quite
easily make others laugh; in the way
your head touches the pillow at night,
and you pray for more beautiful days
like the one that just passed.

Enough of looking for some secret doorway
to a place that will take your breath away.
Magic is here, everywhere—trust me.
And if you just look hard enough,
you will see, within you the most
breathtaking magic resides.

A Poet

When he's had
enough, he gets up
and picks up his pen.
The ink bleeds,
the words flow.
Strip by strip,
he puts his confidence
back on. He smiles
— enough with
feeling small.

This is how
he will change
the world.

The Light That Gives

Make no mistake of thinking
you can ever lose all your magic.
When it is time to put your pen down,
when you stop strumming your guitar,
or dribbling the ball, when you put away
your shoes never to dance again, or when
the brush is retired because you are tired,
because the applause has already died,
your light still shines on. For it is not a candle
to be consumed; your magic is starlight to be

s   a   r
   c   e   e
       t
        t   d

all around.

It will live in every poem and every song
and every art you ever made; in every hall
and every court and every stage you once
owned. And every now and then, someone
somewhere will stumble upon those tiny
specks of you, and start a spark in their
own astounding light.

Aguinaldo

There was a time of innocence,
of dreams, and of simple things.
There was a time when all we had
and all we could give was bliss.

Sixteen years gone
and didn't time just fly by?
I will speak of you not as a father
but as a child—
chubby cheeks, clad in your best clothes,
hair neatly combed
—a split second when life was perfect,
forever frozen in that faded photograph.

Dust

And if I were indeed
just a speck of dust,
infinitesimal
and irrelevant,

at least let me be
the kind that settles
on the windshield glass,
where someone's fingers
will trace for the both of us,

words of quiet declaration,
perhaps in between sighs:

I was here.

Versions

Isn't it ironic how it took all this chaos
to meet all the versions of yourself
you never knew existed, and in them,
find peace.

--pandemic poem #3

Magic of the Modest

Sometimes, it's simply the warmth
of your blanket and the softness
of your pillows at night.

Sometimes, it's a new pen, and you
could swear, you have never found
one that glided and wrote so well.

A cordial smile from a stranger;
a parcel; the way your hair looks
perfect today; cheesecake;
a childhood friend who stayed.

Oh, these little things
and all random, ordinary, joyful things
—gratitude, for all of them.

Meegwetch for the magic of the modest!

* Meegwetch – *Thank you* in Cree (Indigenous group in Canada)

No Other Voice

In the quiet of the night,
just as you embrace the comfort of darkness
and sink in the softness of your sheets,
at last, there is no other voice to listen to
but the beating of your own heart saying,

enough...

       enough...

              enough...

Chasing Silhouettes

It wasn't that
you are not worth it.
You see, all along
you have been chasing silhouettes
—unsure, unclear, indistinct.

Never expect them to stay;
if there is one thing
you know about shadows,
it's that they disappear
in complete darkness.

Shower Thoughts

All these hundred
half-moments of
glorious epiphany
would not compare
to when I realized
I do not need you.

Let's Play a Game...

Put a finger down, for never
will you ever again
chase those who keep running away.

Put a finger down, for never
will you ever again
disrespect yourself by begging
for someone's affection.

Put a finger down, for never
will you ever again
seek validation from those
who do not mean well.

Put a finger down, for never
will you ever again
walk away from who you truly are.

Put a finger down, for never
will you ever again
be blind to notice
those who will die for you.

And now, place your clenched fist
close to your heart and
believe yourself when you say,
Never will I ever again not choose myself.

Splendid Serendipity

I have long given up
searching for things
I cannot find.

Beautiful things turn up
in splendid serendipity.
They come, unannounced,
subtly like shooting stars.

And though sometimes
fleeting, they linger
long after they're gone.

Wednesday

My name is Wednesday,
not the beginning
nor the end.
I am just here
and you might take
me for granted.

But if you ever find me,
please do not look back—
you have come so far.
Do not look too far ahead—
it is still a long way.
Savor me and all
that I can offer.

I am the calm
in the midst
of all this chaos.

Today, you are exactly
where you need to be.

say it, say it proudly
and with utmost
serenity—*I happened*

100%

Not the past,
for you do not live there
anymore.

Not the future,
for it is but a dream
unfulfilled.

You are here—
now,
present in the present,
one hundred percent,
persistent.

Greatest Mess

How many times
have you scolded me
for being clumsy and full of mess.
Would it appease you now
if I say that you are
my life's greatest mess
I'll never want to clean up?

A Galaxy of Our Own

Perhaps sometimes
we aren't supposed to fathom
stars into constellations.

Perhaps there are nights
we just need to stare at them
in all their scattered glory.

There is beauty in chaos
—in things we don't understand,
in questions left unanswered.

You and I are stars in our own
cluttered, confusing galaxy.

We are each other's chaos.
We are each other's peace.

I have learned to listen
to your unsaid words.
I have befriended
your sweet
silence.

Turns

When I am frail
I know
you will be strong.
When you find it
unbearable
I will carry it for you.

No, my love,
we do not make
each other strong.
We take turns
being strong
for each other.

Inside our embrace,
there is enough space
for weakness.

Tawhay

I hang my keys on the wall as I get home,
take off my shoes, undress myself from Today,
wash all What Could Have Beens off my skin,
and put on a pair of plain, simple What Is.
I am learning to be comfortable sleeping in them.

A Life Lived

If I'm lucky enough
to reach the autumn
of my life, I wish
that each falling leaf
be a photograph—
a snapshot of a life
lived not in dullness
but in all colors bright.

And when all is done,
there will be nothing
left of me.
But wasn't that beautiful?
someone will proclaim
with their glittering eyes.

It was. It really was.

An Artist's Vow

And if we're only ever remembered,
if we're only as good as our last,
let me be like the trees in the fall,
and give you one final spectacular show.

The Uprooting

They say it as though it isn't possible to leave some parts
of us behind, as though when we seek for another soil
in which to thrive, we pluck our lives from the ground,
as though we won't survive with just what we take with us.

Uprooting is not the word. Back home there is a plant
whose name you cannot say without twisting your tongue.
Tear one leaf or cut one tender branch, throw it wherever
and it will grow roots of its own, like the only thing it ever
knows is to live, to grow, to uprise.

We are made of this plant, those of us who leave our native
land. Every place we go is every place to grow. We cling to
a new soil while new leaves sprout from every piece of us.

But the more our new leaves reach for the sky, the deeper
our old roots dig in the ground, as if to keep us steady, as if
to keep us from toppling down, perhaps because somehow,
they still hold us, in more ways than we understand.

Some say the world is a garden and perhaps it is, but one thing
is for sure—we will grow wherever, but we will always long
for the taste of the earth from which we first sprang.

Snow Flower

And when you find a snow flower
in the dead of winter, tell yourself,
I, too, am strong, beautiful, resilient.

Homecoming

On days when it feels like
you have lost yourself,
remember, you were saltwater
before you became rain.

In times when confusion
turns you into hurricane,
come home to the ocean.
When water and water mix,
it will feel like you never
left in the first place.

For nothing says welcome back
better than how ripples rise
into waves at the sight of you
to see who gets the honor
of embracing you first.

Remember,
you have always been
part of this vastness.

A Prayer

If it so happens that I will never again
cross paths with the ones I have hurt
to make amends and apologize,
may the universe shower them first,
with love and happiness, before myself.

Southpaw Society

We are the awkward bunch. The anomaly. Clumsy, little, mysterious rarity. We are the ten percent. The dark side. Sinister biological peculiarity. This right-handed world likes to wonder, "Why are you still even here?" It hasn't always been kind. But we have known that this world was not built for us. We have known ever since we were a child when, for the very first time we wrote our names, it had to be with the "proper hand", when we were told the left is our dirty hand. It is a righty, righty world. And we don't belong here.

So we built our own. We know we will never be friends with scissors and the armchair will always make us feel like an uninvited guest at someone's party. Give us a can opener and we will give you disaster. Language hasn't been any kinder either. Is it any surprise to you that the word "left" literally means "weak"? We don't need any of that.

So we built our own. It is a world where cut paper need not be perfect. Perfection is boring, anyway; a world where left arms are always much bigger, always much stronger than the right; a world where everything is done in reverse. Righty tighty, lefty loosy. Make no mistake. This world of ours doesn't fall apart easily.

Because even as they hate, we love. WE. ARE. NOT. WEAK.

We are gentle. And we always love gently. To the ones who
still believe in romance we want to say:

Love a lefty and you will never have to worry—
about useless fights, falling short, not measuring up.
We were born to compromise. In the game of
meet-me-halfway, we damn well excel! And if you
ever need a hand to hold, come take my left one.
It is much stronger than any hand you have ever held.
It had to be. Trust me, it will never give up on you.
It will never let you go.

And though we never got the hang of giving our right
shoulders when we hug, we hug as tightly, anyway.
The smudge on our pinky finger is a stamp we proudly
carry — of a lover who loves way too deeply. We will
write you poems. No matter how much the ink stains,
we will write about you. The world may forget about us
but we will make sure it will remember you.

You see, we've been dancing along to this music called
life with our two left feet. Never in the groove, always
tripping and stumbling, always having to look around
to see what others are doing. Then we do the opposite
way. We have mastered the art of adjusting.

So when the world starts to make us feel cheated
as it is bound to do, when we start to feel
that life is unfair, trust that we will remember

to unclench our fist; let go of that indignance.

We will look at the palm of our left-handed glory.
We have been this way for five thousand years.
We'll get through five thousand more.
All our life we were simply meant to survive.
And yet we stood out.

Still

If life is nothing but a series of coincidences,
I am glad I am here now, by chance,
doing what I do, by accident, and that
in that one completely serendipitous moment,

I met you.

And wouldn't you agree, it is still altogether
a wonderful life of spontaneity?

Acceptance Speech

Today,
above all things,
I accept
who I am
and all
the greatness
within me.

I promise,
all days before me
will become faded memory
of a time you didn't know love.

When you met
my eyes for the first time,
I saw in yours a familiar glance,
and I was almost sure, somewhere before,
in my poems or in another lifetime,
we have stared at each other
a thousand times.

Compass

And we could spend
a lifetime navigating,
only to realize, we are
each other's home.

Born to Weather

Drop your raincoat;
leave your boots behind.
All you need are us
and the promise that when
the rain becomes too heavy
we can't even open our eyes,
it's your hands I will always find.

That's all it takes to know
we were born to weather
the strongest storm.

The Falling

Day by day
piece by piece
slowly, soundlessly
like a tree shedding leaves
I fall for you.

Sound of Love

If someday
somebody asks,
*What sound
did it make for you,
the falling in love?*

I will smile and say,
I used to think
it would be a loud
thumping of the heart,
but it was the crackle
of leaves being crushed
by two pairs of feet
walking side by side.

Summer Rain

You are the summer rain
that came just as I
have made plans for the day.
But by all means
pour down a little more
because my love,
I think I'll never want
to stop dancing.

At a Standstill

Every time I let
my palms meet
at the tiny space between
my nose and my lips
you ask me what
I'm praying for.

I have told you long ago
it's just one of my quirks,
my weird little ways.
But still I say,
"That time stand still."
You hug me, body against my back,
your arms tracing mine.

"What are you praying for?" I ask.
And you hold my hands
tighter in response.
Moments like this, indeed,
time stands still.

In the Phone Booth

I think I can't thank
the rain enough
for drowning the sound
of my pounding heart.

In the phone booth,
that afternoon we were alone,
I had no excuse
if you asked me what
the jitter was all about.

The Present

You are a present
wrapped ever so perfectly.
And all at once, I knew
you are what I asked for.

But shouldn't I know better than
to unwrap you with frenzied eagerness
only to end up tearing you apart?

There was a reader who once said
in half-spoken admiration, flipping a page
he lingered on for so long:

*Oh, what beauty there is
in taking things slow.*

Breaths of Hope

I promise to multiply
breaths of hope you give,
and blow each one
on dandelion seeds
for everyone to take.

Jealous

I'm jealous of your eyes—
not by the way they seem
to shine with childlike charm
but by how they hold stories of you
I have yet to know.

If I could see through
those eyes for a day
I want them to show me
your saddest, worst days.
I want your heartaches
to be my heartaches —
so that I may share half the pain,
so that I may love you better,
so that someday
I may be able to tell you
those eyes shall never see
sad days again.

Sunshower

I want to be out
in a sunshower with you,
stare at you
under the glitter waterfall.

I'd take you to the woods.
Cold and drenched,
we'll find a procession—
a wedding of beasts.

This, I'd say, and ours,
is the romance
this summer rain brings.

Sacred

Promise is a sacred word, you said.
And so in the name of all that is sacred,
today and in civilizations past,
I promise that I will let you grow
however you want.

You may taste the world
with the palate of a child,
pure and innocent in delight.
You may wish to sail alone
across the ocean of your fears.
You may choose to wander.
You may choose to walk away.

And when you've filled your soul
with enough wisdom the world could give,
you can turn around and count
your steps back with the certainty
that at the end of the very last footprint
I'd still be there, waiting for your return.

Manic Pixie

I've been tinkering
with far too many recipes,
one too many spices,
always either too much
or too little of something,
until you came along
and showed me how
to rightly ginger up
this bland, ordinary life.

Cartography Lesson

Aren't you just
a conqueror in love,
my body your map
and the tip of
your finger a pen,
marking your territory—
all the places
you have loved me.

Magicians

Are you ready
to begin the show?
We will leave everyone
in awe of our love,
make them believe
there is no trick,
just pure magic.

Sunshine

Sunshine smile
and sparkly eyes—
how could you
possibly hold
that much light?

When you walk around
with all your warmth,
I feel it in my skin
and I swear,
I could not
be more alive.

The Magic of True Friendship

Years
and oceans
apart,
and so much
life in between.

But I know
no matter how far,
no matter how long,
I could talk to you
again, as though
not a day went by.

On Childhood Friends

What love
is more spontaneous
than that which sprang
from the innocence
of childhood,
from shared wonder
about what was once
a tiny world.

Sweet Solace

This world is too loud for me.
Shelter me with your love—
in all the splendid silence of it.

Snow Crystal

I have known you from a distance
long enough to know
you never liked all things warm.

I know everything about you.
I know your shape
and every which way you shine.

You could fall among a mountain
of snow and I would
still recognize you—you gentle,

fragile miracle, you—pure and
one of a kind.
I wish there was a way I could

hold you, ever so tenderly, without
destroying your beauty,
without you melting in my hands.

Snow Crystal's Response to Its Admirer

I do not care about my beauty,
for I was never made to last, anyway.
I would gladly collapse,
disintegrate into nothingness,
if it meant that for once, I would
know how it feels to be warm.

It isn't true I do not like warmth.
I was never afraid of melting.
I am terrified of melting in the wrong hands.

The Art of Mending

I come to you incomplete.
The path that led me here
was not easy, and somewhere,
I lost some of me.

So forgive me if this is all
I could ever give, but please
take all the pieces left of me.
Find where they fit
in all the broken parts of you.

Maybe we will always stay
broken just as we are,
but maybe,
maybe we can learn
the art of mending.

Maybe there is a way
to hold each other
and feel whole again.

Unified

Fingerprints
dissolving between
interlacing hands;
you and me,
we become one.

Covenants

And he said to him,
Your love for me is wonderful;
your soul is knit to mine.
He armored him
with his own.
He loved him as himself.

And she said to her,
Where you go I will go,
and where you stay I will stay.
She cleaved unto her
like Adam clung to Eve.
Her home became her home.

If there is God
who invented love,
or is love, Himself,
then he must also be
the god of souls knit
and bodies cleaving
unto each other.

So Much Love, So Little Time

It is only when
I am with you
that I am inclined
to believe in a lifetime
beyond this one.

Our life here now
is but a blink of an eye,
and I am always
running out of time
loving you.

Last Frontiers

There are places

           in me,

and places

           in you

beyond reaching.

There are always ocean floors
that sunlight   cannot touch,
caves i̶m̶p̶e̶n̶e̶t̶r̶a̶b̶l̶e̶ and
mountain peaks that are want of

                 g.

              n

           i

         b

      m

    i

   l

 c

Your last frontiers are yours;
my last hidden ones are mine,
and those we should never cross,
if only to preserve our mystery.

But in all the ones we invite
each other in, I'll always meet
you there, by the doorstep, or
halfway, or at the edge, if you
promise you will do the same.

Lost, with you,
in this wilderness
that is life,
and for once
I am not afraid.

Metal to Gold

I came to show you
what I did with all the bullets
I have been collecting.

Call me alchemist, for these
wings of gold, unlike anything
you've ever seen before,
from them I have fashioned.

I came to tell you
I am flying away from here,
to a place where I finally belong.
I wanted to know, if I tell you
I will never return,
would you hold my hand
and disappear with me?

And if not, watch me unfurl
my wings as I fly.
Tell people about this day,
tell them,

      I am free.

acknowledgments

In the process of completing this work, I developed a renewed appreciation for Sufi poetry, all thanks to the meditative readings on YouTube that gave me the calmness I needed to get things done. I thank the Sufi poets for the wisdom of their words.

I am also grateful to Tyler Knott Gregson, my favorite poet, for the inspiration. You have greatly influenced my writing style.

Thank you, Angela Dianne Agustin, for breathing life into my poems through your illustrations. Thank you, Van Piedad, for designing the cover image and capturing the essence of the concept of this book. It was a pleasure working with both of you.

Finally, and most importantly, thank you to all my friends to whom I "manifested" this book when it was just an idea. You know who you are. I appreciate all your support. Thank you for believing in my magic.

about the author

r.c. perez is a Filipino-Canadian poet and teacher. He was born and raised in a rural town in the Philippines and is now based in Toronto. He started sharing his work in 2020 through Instagram. He writes in simple words about simple subjects in an attempt to embody his concept of magic of the modest—beauty in simplicity. This book is his debut collection of poetry. When not writing, he is busy with baking or origami. He is a pineapple-on-pizza apologist.

Made in the USA
Middletown, DE
26 May 2021